Welcome to the World
as seen through my Eyes

From The Other Side

Poetry and Short Stories

Neall Ryon

BALBOA.
PRESS
A DIVISION OF HAY HOUSE

Balboa Press books may be ordered through booksellers or by contacting:

Balboa Press
A Division of Hay House
1663 Liberty Drive
Bloomington, IN 47403
www.balboapress.com
1 (877) 407-4847

Photo credits
Reciting poetry: Janet Kvamman, PlanetJanet Creations:
Cover photograph: Neall Ryon. (taken at 37,000 feet flying over Iceland looking to the sun breaking the horizon over Norway.)

Print information available on the last page.

ISBN: 978-1-9822-3418-8 (sc)
ISBN: 978-1-9822-3421-8 (e)

Balboa Press rev. date: 09/25/2019

Gratitude

There are many that I want to thank and offer my deepest appreciation. Among others they include, Past Poet Laureate of New Westminster; Candice James, for opening the door to my sharing my poetry and her acknowledgment of the potential poet in me. Also, I express my appreciation to Janet Kvammen, Vice-President of the Royal City Literary Arts Society and the many poets and story writers within the writers community of New Westminster and Vancouver B.C. for their encouragement.

A sincere thank you to all those who told me this work needed to be published and to my best friend Michelle who continued to encourage me with patient support. Thank you, all.

Dedication

This Book is dedicated to the infinite wisdom expressed in the many books I have read and experiences of life and to the thousand and one teachers I have met on my way to now.

I also dedicate this book to my Grandchildren; Benjamin and Emily. May the stories you invent create fulfilling lives overflowing with love and laughter.

This Book

This book is about life. Your life, my life and the compassion we need to recognize that we are all one. We are all the same soul having seven billion variations on the experience called "my life."

The one absolute that every person has in common with every other person on the face of this Earth is our humanity. Our humanity seeks the expression of our emotions and the most important of all of our emotions is love. Love is nurturing, love is healing, and the need for love is the deepest longing within each of us.

The poems and short stories in this book are written with the intent of conveying this idea. No matter who we are our emotions are the background noise that drives each of our lives. For good or evil the direction of our lives is dictated to us by our emotional needs. We will lie for love, steal for love, die for love and regrettably we may even harm others for love.

We may try to rationalize our behaviour but underlying all of our actions is the question: "How do we fulfill our need to feel loved?" It turns out that we have seven billion ways of doing just that.

Contents

Part Four
Poetry

Part Five
Stories

Part One

A Story

From the Other Side

I'd rather live as if God exists and find out that He doesn't than to live as if he doesn't exist and to find out He does.

Blaise Pascal circa 1648

From the Other Side

Chapter One

It was formless. That is, without matter in any form. Not drifting in space like some detached entity but a collected energy. A genderless aura of coherent thought that existed outside of the space/time continuum occupying neither space nor time. None the less, this conscious thought existed as clearly as you or I.

Thought was preparing to incarnate into physical form and was reviewing the list of objectives that defined its purpose to be born into a human body. The list included experiences that it will have in its future life. Thought believed those listed experiences would support achieving specific objectives that will benefit the growth of human kind towards consciousness. The time to merge with the soon to be born was drawing near.

Thought was not alone. It felt the presence of a serene energy.

Thought spoke to Awareness; "I deeply appreciate the chance to reincarnate and experience the absolute thrill it is to experience physical form. With the incredible range of beauty offered there, the material realm is awesome. As well as the beauty of the sights, there are smells, textures, tastes, and the sensations from physical contact as well as the emotional connections with others. It is a feast of sensation."

He paused, distracted by the thought of such pleasures; "My merging with this human form is not only about the physical pleasures but offers the chance to add loving energy to both worlds; the material world and this one, the etheric realm. I have enjoyed this gift many times before and in fact, I have lost count. Have you a memory of how often I have done this?"

Awareness responded, "Think back several thousand millennia. Our journey began with the combining of the animal with spirit energy

We needed a physical form that has the capacity to learn so we selected an anthropoidal animal that we could teach. It began first as recognition of others and then recognition of self.

In that recognition was the nascent emergence of love. You asked then how you could help the space/time creature to grow mentally, emotionally and spiritually. Growth in these three areas is the basis for the development of love and compassion that is the root of consciousness. You are continuing that process that you began several thousand incarnations past.

Awareness continued; "Humans have made tremendous improvements since the beginning of self-recognition and there are still many opportunities for them to grow emotionally and spiritually. You get the opportunity to design whatever life path you believe will support that effort."

Thought brightened and asked; "You mean I can have any kind of life? I get to pick and choose? Hey, line me up for one of those silver spoon specials! I'll start with a few million shekels and we can go from there."

Ignoring Thoughts' attempt at humour, Awareness queried, "Will a Silver-spoon start help you achieve the objectives you have designed? You know that's not where you're headed."

Feigning disappointment Thought replied, "I suspect not. There's a whole lot of experiences in a silver spoon style of life that I don't think would be useful to my objectives, especially the fact the silver spoon experience can totally destroy the human's self-esteem. To have the confidence to grow emotionally and spiritually, humans need challenges. They get bored easily and are constantly seeking novelty. They need something to stretch them, something to push against or they tend to drift aimlessly, seeking a life that has meaning."

Awareness asked, "Is the design of your next life now cast in stone?"

Thought, pondered for a moment of non-existent time, "Yes, it is pretty much completed. I will be born a boy to an unwed teenaged girl who understands that human life is a gift.

Circumstances and pressure from others will cause her to choose to adopt me out to others right from the moment of our birthing. These experiences will give several humans opportunities to grow into greater compassion and love. They will be given opportunities to release their guilt and shame regarding their repressive ideas about proper behaviour and learn to offer compassion to others for the sometimes emotionally painful experiences of being in-body."

Thought continued, "I have tried to but I can't seem to remember my last birthing." The impending baby boy asked; "Does it hurt to be born? For the baby I mean?"

Awareness' responded, "No. Incarnate pain is essentially a function of memory. It will take some short time to bring together all the synapses and cognition connections to build a memory of what pain is, or isn't.

At the first moment in space/time, you will not have a pain memory to base pain on. When you merge almost everything you know at this moment will be forgotten."

Awareness continued; "There are a few exceptions. You don't need to remember your list of planned experiences or objectives as they are automatically encoded in the genetic structure of the being.

"On occasion, your emotions may remind you to notice opportunities for your listed experiences. These will come as urges to go in a particular direction. If you are really off the mark your feelings can be very powerful and insist you either re-join the plan or leave space/time to reset the direction towards the objectives that you specified in your design."

"You mean I have to physically leave space/time to reset my objectives. If I truly screw up my human conduit will cease to be? It will die."

Knowing Thoughts rebellious nature from past lives, Awareness chuckled at the idea. "No, not necessarily, just learn to stay with your feelings and that will keep you out of deep trouble."

Awareness paused. "But we digress! There are remembered genetic programming and desires for experiences that come along with the human form from its animal origins. These human genetically remembered states rarely come into serious conflict with your objectives, but age and experience should teach you to deal with the animal level memories of the being you will inhabit."

Awareness continued, "Insertion happens automatically and is completed with the first breath of the newborn infant.

Every bit of matter in space/time is conscious of its existence, therefore, life begins at the moment of conception but it is not the first heartbeat that signals the entry of the soul and the beginning of human life. It is the first breath.

All you need to remember as the baby emerges from the female is to breathe. As long as you remain in space/time realm your breath and your feelings are your only connections to this infinite energy realm. Pay attention to your breath."

"It has been proven again and again that experience is the teacher, so you agreed to have experiences that will help the human species progress towards becoming aware. Towards a state of enlightenment that allows humans to let go of the drama that humans thrive on and move to a clear sense of understanding that they are a part of the evolution of the Universe.

For the most part, they have done well but they still require help to find and nurture the love and compassion that is embedded in every one of them from birth."

"Have you completed your own list of objectives?"

Thought responded; "Yes I have and it consists of three primary objectives. I will offer opportunities for several people to learn and to grow in love.

These include opportunities to learn forgiveness for themselves and for others and including my birth parents, their parents and my adoptive parents plus several others I will encounter along the way.

I also plan to produce progeny that will offer opportunities for my own emotional growth in compassion based behaviors and thirdly;

I will work to improve my own energetic vibration in order to add positive energy and increase the spiritual vibration on the planet."

Awareness asked; "What are the experiences that will help you achieve those objectives?"

"I will use many experiences of abandonment, struggles with clear communications with parental behaviors and their struggle to find sanity in the midst of insanity generating stress. The stress created by deviation from societal rigidity and a survival imperative to fit in.

I will utilize the experience of being a single parent of a male child that will offer me the circumstances to learn more about love and compassion. I am looking forward to the adventure I have planned."

"Why did you choose to enter space/time as the male of the species?"

"I did the female soma last time and it was very difficult to find self-esteem. I don't want to repeat that gender anytime soon. It was so hard to have self-respect and empowerment as a female person when societal imperatives mean that the female still does not have equal status with the male of the species. That self-rejection is taught from a very early stage making it difficult to imagine ones, female self, as worthy.

The impossibility of this situation is that the primary caregiver is a female and the initial source of that belief.
Females who are not empowered do not know how to teach their female children to be empowered.

This is slowly changing but I decided the males of this species also need to find emancipation from their own limiting beliefs around what it is to be male, which in turn will allow them to see the female role differently, supporting change in both."

Awareness interrupted, "I see your host is preparing to be born. I wish you a joyous adventure and success in gaining your objectives. Now go! It is time."

Chapter Two

The doctor held the newborn infant up by his ankles so as to clear his airways of amniotic fluids. At that moment, the baby, having been rudely extracted from its warm, nurturing, inner sanctum, shuddered and inhaled his first breath.

Part Two

Poetry

knowing others is intelligence;
knowing yourself is wisdom.

Laozi (Lao Tzu)
Circa 530 BCE

The Poet

The poet responds to a voice that reaches down to us
from the other side. It emerges down through the noise
and clatter of the mind and speaks to the poet.
When that voice gets shared we call that poetry
and them that give utterance to the gift, we call them poets.

The voice that speaks through the poet transforms a
simple wordsmith into a profound speaker of wisdom.
One who puts pen to paper so that all may hear the insight and
wisdom that springs forth from the offerings of that voice.

Words waft and weave in the air emanated from the poet,
expressed with the intent to share a recognition
of our common humanity.
The poet expounds the truths of our common problem of being
half animal full of wants and needs as well as half Spirit
full of prayers and chants.

At the beginning of time, the voice spoke the poem
around the fire and then retold the story
painted onto the walls of caves.
That voice tells and retells of the epic journey of
humanity, repeated from eons upon eons past.

The voice utters words, speaking from the deepest darkest part
of our memory. Beyond conscious thinking, but recognized
by our collective memory.
That poetic voice can be understood by every
human being in this world without regard to race,
colour, ethnicity, gender or religious belief.

The Poetry speaks to everyone as we all share a
common memory emerging from a distant past.
It is the same voice that spoke to the poets who wrote; The
Iliad, The Odyssey, and The Epic of Gilgamesh, The Rhyme
of the Ancient Mariner, and Ozymandias; King of Kings.

It is the voice that spoke to our fore-bearers and we recognize
a few of their names; Ovid, Homer, Rumi, Shelly and Tagore.
Untold others in every language in every time, Poets speak
to us of our common ancestry from when we became aware
that life is a series of experiences of tragedy and of joy.

Poets share in a million ways the joys and the tragedies
that we all recognize.
A tale of heartbreak and horror; of joy and ecstasy,
Poets share the story of what it is to be human
a journey common to us all.

---

a haiku

in meditation
a stillness lies in waiting
with a gift of peace

It's All Music

Quantum Physics tells us that everything
in the Universe is of vibrating strings.
To be in vibration means to have a frequency and a frequency
is a tone, the essence of music. Everything is a vibrating tone
in the grand composition that is the music of the Universe.
That music plays out as vibrations that we translate
into a physical experience.
It's all Music.

Music is not just the perfect compositions
of Bach, Beethoven and Brahms.
Nor is it the discordant sounds of
Shostakovich or Ornette Coleman.
Music is more than the sweet sounds of a
Heifetz violin or a silky smooth Stan Getz samba
Everything is music in the perfection of the
vibrations sung to us by the Universe.
It's all Music.

Senses translate the vibration of sight sound, taste and
touch as material things but each begins as a tone
The music that is food appears in our mouth as taste.
Salty, sweet, bitter are all different songs.
The music that is sight, on its journey to our eyes, is
a vibrating range of colours that we select from. The
music that is sound matches the frequencies
that we translate with our ears.
But everything that we experience begins
its journey to us as music.
It's all Music.

The stars offer celestial music as a chorus of the
inconceivable vastness of this Universe.
The music of the moon croons an ancient lullaby
we all recognize from eons past.

The music that is water is not the sound
of the ripples in the stream, nor the crashing of its
waves. Water is the music of our Mothers heartbeat
from the very beginnings of our creation here on earth.
It's all Music.

We hear the song of the crow as a cawing,
but it is music from the animal kingdom,
those with whom we share this planet.
The sparrow's song, the whale's song,
the cry of the eagle,
All sing Rejoice! Rejoice in the music that is
being played by the Universe, just for us.
It's all Music!

---

a haiku

where does world peace grow?
in the garden you planted.
the one in your heart.

Thinking the Story

The tribe says we need to identify as separate
so that we survive.
Customs, traditions and religion are all
expressions of the tribe.
These barriers create separation, divergent views
and blindness to the oneness of all things.

All data are that this Universe burst forth
from one single point.
Accordingly every existing particle of this Universe
is inseparably co-joined with every other
particle of the Universe.
Our existence is the manifested consciousness of that
enchanted singularity.

The drama that is life is played out
in this dream we call reality.
Our life arises from the thoughts
and emotions we hold as true.
And by recognizing the experience
for what it is; our story.

The truth of our experience emerges out of the story
we tell ourselves.
We alone are the creator of the Universe that
manifests before us.
Choosing the reality we want comes from vanquishing those
emotions that select for other than the happiness we want.
But ancestral survival rules demand that we
suppress all but the tribal beliefs.

The tribe fears our thoughts and emotions
and dictates to have control of them.
And yet the power of our hidden thoughts
and hidden emotions
Are guaranteed to manifest all the sadness or all
the happiness we experience in life.

Wanting

I want peace!
What do I do daily to engender peace in my heart?

I want to be loved!
What were the experiences where I learned to love?

I want to be forgiven for my mistakes.
How well do I forgive others for their humanity?

I want to be happy
Am I content with what I have or is more my goal?

I want to be healthy
How well have I listened to my dis-ease?

I want to feel successful.
On whose scale do I measure my success?

What pleases my inner spirit?
What medium do I use to express my creativity?

I want peace in the world
What action do I take and to express that desire?

If it is to be, it's up to me, rings hollow.
I expect these gifts to be delivered to my door
tomorrow morning by FedEx.

---

a thought

have you caught on yet to the fact that life is just a play,
where; we are the audience and
we are the charters in the play and
we are the playwrights who write the play

There's Room Here

Everyone is the same self, draped in differences.
Different colours, different languages, different bodies,
different experiences but we all share one humanity.
No matter what makes you different.
There is room here for you.

Everyone is imperfect; everyone is wounded.
Perhaps we are here to learn that the true evil
in the world is our judgment that others are different.
No matter how or who you are in this world;
There is room here for you.

Male or female, crippled or whole,
advantaged or disadvantaged,
quick or slow, typical or unusual,
we are all challenged by being alive.
And in the heart, we all share the same desire
to be loved and accepted.
Try to remember that in this wondrous
spectrum of diversity;
There is room here for you.

There are those among us who do not see
the same humanity in everyone.
Some are always willing to tell you how
you don't measure up,
to standards set by those blind
to their own humanity.
Some can be harsh and mean in their judgments
so it's hard to remember;
That there is room here for them as well.

It must be painful for them
when they get glimpses of their own imperfections.
They can only see through judgmental eyes
and have not yet learned
that inner peace comes with loving
our common humanity.
They seem to be taking forever to learn acceptance
of the other. Even yet;
There is room here for them as well.

Fear of the unknown, fear of differences,
fear of not being accepted.
Not feeling loved, not feeling valued,
not feeling safe, opens the doorway to fear.
We all share an ancestral monkey nature
that we need to be loved to survive.
World peace can begin when we all become
aware; There is room here for us all.

---

a thought

there are those of us that are so good at judging others
that we can find them guilty
without even knowing what they did.

On The Train

I am the impeccably dressed 30 something woman
with small wrinkles at the corners of her eyes
signifying the beginning of her journey into maturity

I am the unkempt tramp in a coat far too warm
for the time of year, toting a green plastic
garbage bag that clanks of empty cans

I am the dark haired teenager, her in-vogue jeans
ripped at the knees thumbs rapidly tapping
onto the keyboard of her mobile.

I am the man in the red and white hockey sweater
telling a young boy about last night's game
and who made the winning goal.

I am the old man, hands resting on his cane
looking out the window
watching the passing scene.

I am the teenaged boy and the teenaged girl
clinging to each other
enjoying the physical closeness of lovers.

I am the dark blue suit talking on his phone.
touching the knot of his tie
while checking the map of stations.

I am the loud woman with the smokers cough
her darting eyes seeking to confirm
that she is the center of attention.

I am the black man in dirty boots and overalls
carrying his lunch pail
and his construction hard hat.

I am the musician reading the musical score
as the fingers of his left hand
play the notes on his knee.

I am my best friend and I am my worst enemy
I am the best of us and
I am the worst of us.

I have a piece of everyone in me and everyone
has some aspect of me in them
All are reflections of the humanity
that is written in our hearts.

---

a thought

i always like to take a different path home
this increases the probability
of having a new experience
or of starting a new adventure.
aren't those the reasons we came here in the first place

Voices of our Heritage

How far back do the voices of our heritage go?
From how far back do the voices go that speak to us today.
Do the voices of creatures long extinct
still, speak to us of worlds no longer existing?

We are evolving creatures genetically anchored
in the past while striving to enter the future.
How many generations still speak to us
as we rush headlong into a different world?
New technologies, climate change, transmuted
foods, different ways of war.

We are harnessed to the mists of times past through
our DNA not evolving at a speed to match
the progression of our creativity
as we create a future of species yet unborn.
We are humankind carrying the history of yesterday
in these bodies.

Struggling to change and grow with thousands
upon thousands of voices at our backs.
Dead voices that can't evolve and a drag
to slow our striving to assimilate the future.
Our creativity, once our benefactor,
is now threatening our existence.

And we can only ride the wave and pray this path
is not the road to extinction
as it has been for many of the creatures
from which we have emerged. What will become of
this wonderland of creativity, this Earth, our Gaia?
Will Bits and Bytes of data be the requiem
posted on Facebook about our extinction?
Or can we reinvent ourselves to reclaim the garden
that was once ours.

a thought

when adventure beckons
and you hear a voice inside
that says; "You can't do that."
fire the negative cheerleader;
trust that you will be OK
and "Go for it.!".

a haiku

if parting be sweet
my sorrow tells truth to me
the pain is bitter

a haiku

in my memory
the river of my youth still flows
past my cabin door

The Church with No Roof.

A boy stood at the doorway to the church with no roof.
It also had no windows
it also had no doors.
The walls still stood but between them lay the rubble.
Just yesterday it was a whole church; with
a roof and windows and doors.

He had walked by here just yesterday on his way to school
as he does every day on his way to school.
Just yesterday it was a whole church with a roof
and windows and doors
Just yesterday his world was a whole world
that had roofs and windows and doors.

Just yesterday he had a Father
that proudly he marched alongside.
as the soldiers, two by two,
passed the church and boarded their train to Fate.
But this day is different for the church has no roof
and he is no longer secure knowing where Father is.
Just yesterday his pride was whole; with the
certainty of a roof, and windows and doors.

Mother says he is safe in the underground
but he feels his Mother's fear.
Fear that teaches him to be afraid of those he knows not.
The confusion of emotion inside with love for some
and vengeful rage at others.
He dare not think they hate him so,
and wish his family dead.
Just yesterday his emotions were whole
with a roof and windows and doors.

He has a place inside where he hides
the fear-filled feelings.
The uncertainty of existence must not show
He dare not think what horrors might befall him
as he sleeps
He dare not ask, "Why do the other hate us so?"
When just yesterday his love was whole
with a roof, and windows and doors.

His fleeting thoughts "I don't want my Dad to be dead
I don't want the bombs to hurt my Mom.
I need to protect her. There is only one Mother
and one Father allowed per family.
All the rest are strangers.
Just yesterday this family was whole;
with a roof and windows and doors.

He lives on a street where the houses have roofs
and windows and doors to keep out the dampness and the cold.
Just yesterday he had a Mom and Dad
to holiday with and be safe.
but today brings the knowledge,
his world has been bombed.
While just yesterday this world was whole
with a roof, and windows and doors.

It is the same world but his view has been shifted
this child's soul has been hurt,
the world is now unsafe
It is a place where bombs are dropped
with the intention of killing and destroying.
Just yesterday this church was a whole church
with a roof, and windows and doors.

For a moment, I was that boy as I stood before the
entrance to the church in Portsmouth, England.
Thinking of the child who stood in this
experience of learning.
At the entrance to the church
with no roof, no windows and no doors.

Stand in front of any church or temple or mosque.
and imagine it with no roof and no windows and no doors.
Imagine any boy or girl in any nation
in any culture in any language
standing there, where just yesterday for them
their world was whole;
with roofs, and windows and doors.

---

a thought

in every experience, both good and bad.
life guarantees there is a gift.
but sometimes one has to search to find it.

Erasure

The butterfly cannot see the beauty of its wings.
But in the hologram that is the mind of God
every detail is captured to perfection.

Every word ever spoken, every word ever written,
every thought, however brief, and every emotion ever raised
are added to the infinite capacity of this Universe to remember.

Every moment of every day that exists
is a part of the space/time continuum
that our knowledge comprehends so little of.

Erasure of what existed can never be.
The poem once written can be altered
But; however brief the moment, if it ever was, it still is.

All is energy and energy exists without closure.
The decay of now is captured in Brahmaputra never erased.
Every joy, every regret, every life, every
poem persists without end.

And the ceaseless eyes of our soul
captures the data of our existence
to post it on the wall of the black hole we call the Universe.

---

a thought

love everything you have; you've created it.
if you want to change it; love it even more.
then it can show you the gift it has for you.

Desire is a Fundamental Particle

I am so blessed.
I have wall to wall everything I need; yet, still I want.
I have unbounded desire for newness, for novelty,
for something more.

What is it I am still seeking?
to be more loved? to be more fulfilled?
or to add to my inventory of life's experiences.

What is it that causes my body to seek nourishment?
The energy needs of the body as used up the nutrients
from an earlier meal.
And now wants to be replenished.

What is it that causes me to seek something more?
Is it because the life energy that feeds me has been used up
and my desire for novelty is a desire for more of life's energies?

One of the secret truths about life is that
although we seek shelter in sameness and repetition
our hunger for experience
empowers us to spurn the safety of numbness.

Wanting more is the genesis by which life
was created in the beginning.
We are responding to the prime directive of the Universe
to have experiences that provide us with life's energy.

Wanting to learn and to grow is the essence of Spirit
that resides within.
We are just another stepping stone in the evolution of the
Universe and the desire for more is the fundamental
particle that keeps it all going.

The Courage to Fear

It takes courage to allow the fear;
   so that the truth can be felt.
      It takes courage to speak;
         so that the truth can be heard.
            It takes courage to heal;
               so that the truth can be seen.

I speak because the words need to be spoken
   I speak them with heart impassioned force
      I speak them out loud to be heard
         by the humanity that is common to all of us.
            The commonality to everyone in the world is
               that we are imperfect and impermanent.

Within each of us is a spark of recognition
   to this commonality that is felt within the hearts of all.
      For at the moment we recognize our humanity,
         we will connect with love as a reward for our courage
            We will never be alone when we reach out with love
               which begins with the courage to allow the fear.

---

a thought

my mind is always listening
to what I say
so I'm very careful what I tell it

Wholeness

Loneliness is a wound we all carry.
A psychic wound sense of loss that resides within each of
us. A sadness that arises from the loss of the wholeness
we once knew.

Life in the world will never be as satisfying
as life in the uterus where all our needs were met.
That separation from the womb at birth
is humanity's common trauma

Is it the oneness we once felt within our mother's womb;
or is it the despair we feel from the separation
of our soul from the Universal source of love
we mistakenly refer to as God.

When we are born we enter a world
of conditions and judgments.
Behave and I will approve of you
misbehave and I will withdraw my love of you.

This world manipulates us thru the application or
denial of love. Separation from wholeness
and the certainty of unconditional love
is the existential wound we all carry.

Rather than teach self-appreciation and responsibility
the edict of civilization is a carrot and stick approach.
Compounded by our lack of knowledge
of how to love unconditionally

Until the time to return to the womb of wholeness,
the time when we pay the ferryboat-man
the payment we all make for having been given the gift
of life and he returns us to the place of wholeness
from whence we all came.

No Such Thing

In ordinary world time there is no such thing as silence,
only infinitely small moments between thoughts.
By stretching those tiny spaces
one can hear the silence.
That's what meditation is for.

In ordinary space/time, there is no such thing as nothing.
Even in empty space, energy enfolds
and unfolds to fill the void.
But in the infinitely small spaces between our experiences
exists the quiet peace of nothingness;
That's what mindfulness is for.

Calm the turbulence of the mind
and open the door to the awareness that
the consciousness of the Universe resides in the void.
Filled with nothing; waiting for whatever
you choose to put there.
This year, may you fill the nothingness with love.

---

a thought

the purpose of entertainment is to distract us
from seeing life the way it is
the purpose of art is to open us to a new view of the world

Birthday

Birth days are the end of a journey, a journey that began
when yin and yang ignited the spark that contains new
life. Sperm and egg meet to form the zygote and with
this process, the Universal act of creation continues.

The division of cells continues while it seeks to find a home.
This living ball of energy looks for a source of nourishment.
Continually changing, our hero of this journey eventually
enters the womb and, with more growth becomes an embryo

Continuing on a voyage of growth and discovery
this being swims in a brine resembling sea water.
From the barest of beginnings, all the while preparing,
the forming child grows and graduates to a fetus.

It grows what resembles gills then discards them.
It grows what resembles a tail that morph into hips and legs.
. And all the while this baby learns from the sounds
and emotions that permeate its environment.

In a chemical soup of water, fetal offerings and glucose,
it learns which emotion accompanies which sound.
It learns which flood of feelings raises a danger sensation
and which pleasing sensation soothes its soul.

Beyond the walls of its confinement lay a
mysterious world of sounds and shadows.
And even though it resists dying to this aquatic world
the drive to be birthed offers no choice.

So here I am! Incomplete and eager to learn
What you will make of me, World,
will be reflected in, what I make of you,
for today is my birthday!

A Birthright

I deserve to be healthy and live a happy life.
I deserve to release all inherited shame and karma.
I deserve to be loved and supported by the Universe.

Others deserve to be forgiven for trespasses against me,
and I deserve to be forgiven for my trespasses against them.
As well, I deserve to be forgiven for trespasses against myself.

I deserve to have others to love,
I deserve to be loved by others,
I deserve to love myself.

I deserve to live in abundance.
I deserve to live in the Eden of my desire.
I deserve to live a full and adventurous life.

And why am I deserving of all of these gifts.
Because it is the birthright of all humanity;
And although I am nobody special, it is my birthright as well.

---

a thought

most everyone I know is aware of the insanity of being
too busy to stop and smell the roses.
but too seldom take the time to heed its call.

In Appreciation

Today is Thanksgiving!
Is there anything I can be thankful for?
Certainly not the dysfunctional consumer society
which we all endure.
Separated from the heart, to call it prosperity
is indeed faint praise.

Certainly not big oil, big pharma, nor big business.
They steam roller over anyone and anything
that gets in the way of their greed.
Which kinda' makes them public enemy number one.

Certainly not the education system which is structured
to paint a million variations of people with the same brush
and then measure them all with the same yardstick.

Certainly not the troubles and turmoil of life
the groundlessness and impermanence that means
life is ever changing
leaving little if anything that one can rely on!

So what am I grateful for?
I am grateful that I live at a time of greatest
prosperity ever created.
I live in a time of the greatest amount of knowledge
available to most everyone.

I am grateful that I enjoy the foods and fruits of many lands
I am grateful that I live in a time when safe passage
is offered in most parts of the world.
Were travel is easy and great distances made small.

I am grateful for the mountains I've climbed
and the beaches I've walked.
I am grateful that much of nature's beauty still exists.
I am grateful for the people and the spirits
that have guided me in this lifetime.

I am grateful for parents who, in spite of their struggles,
gave me and sustained my life.
I am grateful for the myriad of experiences
I've had in this lifetime
and I am grateful for my existence
and for being born into the perfect time and place.

Without Awareness

Without awareness of our emotions
we are robbed of the greater part of life.

Without awareness of our feelings, there is no Mozart,
no Picasso, no Shakespeare
and no beauty in the flowers on the hillside.

Without heart filtered thought to our actions; our
actions can become inflictive and hurtful.

Without awareness of the cheerleader of our choices
we are blind to our own behaviour.

The Melancholy of Wind Blown Grass

The melancholy expression of wind-blown grass.
In stillness, the hissing sadness emanating from rain on the lake.
The sorrowful beauty of moonlight through the trees.
Nature arouses our emotions in a thousand different ways

Something stirs from inside to remind us
we are feeling creatures.
From ecstatic pleasure to heart-wrenching pain
according to our interpretation of the experience. With
the emotions there to remind us that we exist.

We all know the heartbreak of our wounded inner child.
We all know the pain of a thousand cuts, some big, some small.
We all know the sadness of a thousand goodbyes.
And the fear bearing feelings surprise chaos can create.
All are experiences recorded as a part of our emotional world.

Some blows are so severe, forgiveness is hard to find.
But we deal with the sadness and the losses
however we can and move on.
We process the grieving for those gone from this life.
And after the celebration for the dead, we party on.

Emotion through emotion we live these lives.
From the pain of the negatives through to the joys at the pinnacle.
We carry on having life; one experience at a time.
With our emotions as undeniable proof we exist.

Listen

Listen, Listen, Listen.
Listen to the hum of the bee as he gathers the pollen for honey.
Listen to the rain as it beats out a rhythm on the pond.
Listen to the call of the crow
and the swish of her wings as she flies past.
Listen to the babble of the brook,
The wind in the pines.
Listen to the awakening of morning as the sun breaks the horizon,
Listen to the silence of evening as the world begins its rest.
Listen to when my body says no.
And when my heart says yes.
And when I have learned to listen to all of these.

Then I will be ready to speak.

Doorways

Life gives us doorways
Continually offering doorway to experience after
doorway to experience.
Constantly offering the chance to leave our current experience
pass through the doorway that leaves this experience
and enters a new one.

Some doorways we are delighted to choose
while with others we have no choice but to enter still others,
in hindsight, give us experiences we would rather not
but all are guaranteed to change over time.

Loved ones arrive through doorways not of our doing and
loved one's exit through doorways other than our wanting.
Some doorways are chosen for good reason,
others made were not in our highest good.
The view into every doorway of the past reveals our losses,
Every doorway to the future offers the bright light of creativity.

Fires, floods and time take things from us.
Such is the true nature of life.
Some doorways bring love while others bring grief.
But every new doorway offers the
opportunity to create a different vibration.
A chance to stop making the same choices over again
with the expectation of different results.

Find the doorway to yourself
But throw in a lot of love before you enter there.
The doorway to your true self is laden with the mirrors
of our imperfections.
The grace of life is that all doorways offer the possibility
to add love to the outcome.

The Forgotten

Our finger writes our fate in the dust of ages and moves on.
In time the dust returns to cover the traces of our being here.
It is not death that we fear, so much
as the obliteration of the meaning for our existence.

Erasure into non-existence is the enemy of our ego.
"Lest we forget," is a lie. We will be forgotten.
And like Ozymandias, nothing of our gift will remain
as the eternity of time will obliterate all traces of our being here.

Of the millions born that have lived and died
how well do you remember any of them.
The taste of this truth is bitter on my tongue
And I dare not utter what appears to be true.

Entropy demands all traces of my existence will face erasure.
This self-devouring Universe ensures that all will be forgotten.
It may be important to me, that I bring something to the party
yet time will obliterate the absurdity and leavings of my enthusiasm.

Even though it matters now, erasure will begin on my death.
The deeds of a few are remembered but the story is not the person.
And the truth of their existence is distorted into a story.
In the millennium of time, even the famed are ephemeral.

In the face of the oncoming tide of eradication,
my love story is written in the sand of the moment.
And the enormity of my death matters
most to the words that follow "I am…"

In this is an ever-changing, groundless, existence called life,
time is endless and our presence here is truly only now.
The lives of those we knew, now gone, are relegated to the echoes of
our few memories and in the infinite corridors of time,
erasure is the fate for all that is.

The Coin has Four Sides

true to its infinite nature, the coin has four sides:
each side in balance
each side hides a plus and with it hides a minus

each side is an experience that contains
both Yin and Yang; always in balance.
each experience has four sides eternally equal.

each drought has a flood.
each famine has a bounty.
the Universe eternally resets the balance of plus and minus.

as each sunrise has a sunset.
as each birth has a death.
the universe is Libra, constant guardian of balance.

all that is within is without;
all that is without is within.
the Universe is perfection within perfection.

take notice, every time you win something,
you are made to let go of something.
take notice, every time you lose something,
a doorway to something new is opened.
the true nature of life is the coin has four sides.

Through love all that is bitter will be sweet,
Through love all that is copper will be gold,
Through love all dregs will become wine,
Through love all pain will turn to medicine.

<u>Rumi</u>: A Persian poet circa 1250 AD

Part Three

A Story

The Trial

"Justice must not only be done, but must also be seen to be done."

Lord Chief Justice Gordon Hewart
England 1924.

The Trial

Tap, tap; "Is this mike on? *Hi! Morley Sandford here; Welcome to, 'Evolution Observer' where we report news and views on the evolution of the Universe. We are here today in the Etheric realm where souls awaiting birth or rebirth design the life they think will add the experiences that will increase the Universe's awareness of its infinite self.*

"Today we are reporting to you from The High Court of Universal Justice where we are witnessing the conclusion of a trial of stunning significance. A soul has petitioned the court to terminate the foetus to which he has been assigned in favour of a different parental coupling. The plaintiff is asking to experience a life of greater potential so as to make a contribution of value instead of; as the soul described it, a life as fodder for the continuing procreation of low functioning masses."

The other side is the defendant; Eve Knebworth, who is nine weeks pregnant with the incarnate to which the plaintiff has been assigned. She and Adam Knebworth, live within space-time and have testified they are delighted to find themselves about to bring a child into the world. They find the request to abort the child she carries as outrageous.

"Documents previously submitted included all relevant details and we are here at the final hearing where both plaintiff and defendant will argue their respective positions before the High Courts' Justice Solomon.

Court is about to convene. I will leave this microphone on so we can listen in."

"All rise; The High Court of Universal Justice is now in session; All Compassionate Lord Solomon presiding."

Solomon, clothed in red velvet robes trimmed in ermine, mounted the bench and spoke in a voice that sounded like distant thunder: "Bailiff! Please read the requested injunction."

The Bailiff, a robed, grey-haired imaginary energy stood: "Your honour it reads, 'a Soul assigned to a developing embryo has requested the court to direct the carrier of the unborn, defendant, Eve Knebworth, residing within space/time, to abort her pregnancy and that the Plaintive be assigned to parentage of greater potential for influencing the growth of awareness, love and compassion within their progeny'."

Solomon interrupted; "How is the soul plaintiff to be known?"

Counsel for the defendant stood: "Your Honourable Compassionate One, I am Olivia Cromwell, counsel for defendant Knebworth. My client is aware of the child's gender and has named him; Knoll Knebworth, nicknamed, Tobee." Ms. Cromwell continued; "I respectfully submit the defendant vehemently opposes the imposition of such an order and it is her intention is to carry her impregnation to term."

Solomon held up his hand indicating stop; "Advocate please be seated." and with a nod from Solomon, the Bailiff continued;

"The defendant opposes the imposition of such an order from the court on the grounds that she has an unassailable right to motherhood."

Solomon spoke; "Thank you, Bailiff. Will the Court Advocate please confirm the applicable Universal law as regards this injunction?"

The Court Advocate, a bespectacled female energy stood; "Your Lordship there are two compulsory rules that apply. Universal proclamations state that all persons in the space-time continuum have dominion over all aspects concerning their physical bodies. Specific to this injunction, females are masters of their bodies and no external circumstances exist under which she can be compelled to act.

"Regarding the plaintiff, Universal Law states that humans in space-time have the right to manifest a happy, fulfilling life.

The plaintiff claims that right by requesting participation in the parental selection to engender a life of greater potential happiness resulting in a positive contribution to Universal Consciousness.

Court Advocate continued; "In conclusion, whereas litigants are both claiming constitutional rights, this case is; *est officio judici*, meaning it is the obligation of the court to render a decision."

Solomon pondered this information for some time then spoke;

"Thank you Advocate; Court will now hear arguments from the litigants. Plaintive first, followed by the defendant. Soul Tobee please proceed."

Tobee, a soul of unconsolidated energy arose; "Thank you, Lordship. There are more than my and the defendants' rights here at play. Yes, my incarnation into physical form will satisfy Mrs. Knebworth need to procreate but what of the rights of the unborn. Who speaks for the newborn's right to enter space-time into a nurturing, loving safe environment that will foster and support a life of happiness and fulfillment?

On behalf of all children, I claim the right to a productive life with the intention to bring peace and creativity into a world suffering greatly from physical and emotional pain, acts of war, unthinkable violence and untimely death.

"Previously provided evidence of an unhealthy environment foretells the Knebworth's alcoholic, emotionally dysfunctional lifestyle will birth the child; my incarnate, predisposed to the use of drugs, alcohol or other negative behaviours to hide from the pain of an unfulfilling existence.

Alternatively, he will spend a lifetime working to heal the emotional distresses and regrets from a sorrowful childhood. My right to a life of value far outweighs the defendants' desire to birth a child whose contribution will be of little or no value "On behalf of my incarnate and its future life I claim the right to choose loving, nurturing parents who are living fulfilling lives, able to teach unconditional love to their progeny.

I petitioned the court to grant my request so I can contribute positive emotional growth within the Space/time Universe."

Soul Tobee sat, watching Solomon, searching his energy pattern for a reaction. Solomon's eyes had been closed for the latter half of Tobee's submission and remained closed for what seemed an eternity of non-existent time.

Eventually, Solomon looked up; "Thank you Soul Tobee; Court will take an imaginary 10-minute break to review evidentiary documents."

"Reporter Sandford here. There you have it. Plaintive Tobee has outlined his case to force the defendant to abort her pregnancy so it can have a more propitious birth. Tobee provided evidence that the Knebworths live a dysfunctional, self-abusive lifestyle and are therefore unfit to parent a child. He suggested if carried to term his future self will undoubtedly be similarly dysfunctional who will, in turn, produce additional dysfunctional children. A plaintiff-favourable decision here could affect major changes to the parental selection process.

Chapter Two

"All rise." The Bailiff barked. "Court is now in session."

Solomon assumed his place on the bench and turned to Mrs. Knebwort: "Madam; you may reply to the evidence presented by the plaintiff?

Advocate Cromwell stood: "Your Honourable One, we move this case be dismissed on the grounds that it is the Universal right of the female to have total, irrevocable dominion over her body. No speculative damages offered by the defendant can supersede the Universal law of" Eve Knebworth started to rise but it was her voice that rose; "I want my baby! And you can't take him away!

Solomon was quick to gavel with a crack of lightning and a rumble of thunder; "Order! Order! Your Advocate is speaking on your behalf and if you continue to interject I will remove your voice from the proceedings.

She muttered: "Yes honourableness." as she sat.

Advocate Cromwell continued: "In rebuttal to the plaintiffs' injunction, the defendant states she will accept whichever soul enters the unborn but declares the embryo is of her body and cannot be destroyed.

"My client would be deeply bereft at the loss of her baby causing further damage to a life already traumatized by an abusive, alcoholic family of origin and by a life of recreational drugs attempting to escape her. deep; aw, um, emotional; aw, um, wounds" Realizing her plea for sympathy because of childhood trauma, was describing the main argument of her opponent she hesitated...

Solomon waited… then gently coughed "Ahem."

Cromwell brightened; "Yes, your Honour. It is our position that a woman's body is sacrosanct to her decisions and no one can take away that right. Neither this court nor God herself can abrogate that right. We are complete.

Tobee stood, Solomon frowned; "Soul Tobee, you wish to add something?"

"Your Honour, the argument you just heard from Advocate Cromwell is precisely my argument for an order to abort the zygote at this stage.

I do not wish to harm Mrs. Knebwort nor usurp her right to birth me but it is heartbreaking to see another precious life wasted on the trash heap of childhood trauma through toxic parenting. It is my right to have a happy and fulfilling life engendered by functional parenting able to raise children in an environment of unconditional love. I request the court to order my reassignment to an incarnation that will support my goal of sanity. I am complete."

Solomon spoke: "Thank you both for bringing this challenge to the court. As earth time is an important commodity in regard to this matter, I will deliver my determination tomorrow." With a thump of the gavel; "Court is adjourned to ten o'clock tomorrow."

"Morley Sandford here. You have just heard a soul petitioning for the right to be born into a healthy, loving environment. We have also heard from the defendant who claims the right of inviolability of her body and it is her intention to carry the foetus to term.

Candles will burn late into the night as Justice Solomon wrestles with this judicial challenge."

Chapter Three

"All rise;" The High Court of Universal Justice is now in session; the All Compassionate Lord Solomon presiding.

Solomon entered slowly. He climbed the three steps to the bench and surveyed the courtroom. With rich resonate tones he began; "From the beginning of space-time, when creatures first saw themselves as separate individuals apart from the collective oneness of all, this problem of; 'my need supersedes your needs,' has plagued all beings.

When souls incarnate into human form they see themselves as separate individuals and only occasionally function in the highest good for the collective. But we are not here to reinvent the proper order of things but to resolve this one instance of an age-old question 'Does my right to act in my best interest take priority over your right to act in your best interest?'

"Both manifested and unmanifested beings appear to be missing the point. It is not important what one does in a carnate life but how much one takes away from the experiences they have chosen to have within their assigned lifetime.

Remember, all of us choose to incarnate to bring positive and negative experiences to ourselves that are opportunities for spiritual growth; to become aware; to become conscious. Learning to love unconditionally is the true and only purpose of life.

"I will not interfere with the pregnancy. Nor will I abandon Mr. Tobee's request for a fulfilling life.

I hereby obligate the Knebworth's to take steps to learn and become aware that they assume a great responsibility and need to look closely to the needs of the neonate. Find the potential within the child and nurture it. This is the only important responsibility you will have in your entire life. You are hereby directed to take steps to learn to nurture the infants' growth in a healthy, loving environment."

Looking towards Soul Tobee Solomon continued; "I obligate the plaintiff to be born as intended and to search and find a path of healing. Within wounds there are gifts and it is your responsibility to seek them out and in the healing of those gifts, you will find the fulfillment you seek.

In so doing, the wounds of the Universe are also healed. Everyone's only task in life, and the reason we choose to incarnate is to learn unconditional love, first for ourselves and then for others.

"I charge you both, the plaintiff and the defendant with the responsibility to engender unconditional love within the space-time continuum. That is your true raison d'etre.

Court is adjourned!" With a slam of the gavel, His eminence rose and exited the courtroom to the sound of applause.

This is Morley Sandford live from The High Court of Universal Justice where Chief Justice Solomon has again demonstrated his profound wisdom by solving a real-life dichotomy. We hope you enjoyed today's program of news and views of the growing self-awareness in the evolution of the Universe. Join us again next time here at the 'Evolution Observer' where we report news and views on the evolution of the Universe.

Part Four

Poetry

At the touch of a lover; everyone becomes a poet.

Plato circa 400 BCE

Who Is This Voice of Poetry?

Who is this Voice that speaks words in my ear?
My inner ear that hears the emotions
my muse wants me to share.

Those are the words we try to convey to the page
so it delivers the intended emotion and is recognized
by the listener as poetry.

Find the common thread of society and pluck it. The
music from that string will send the vibration
out into the world conveying the feelings.

Aren't we lucky to have such a wide variety of emotions?
It is the job of the Voice to recognize and express
those feelings in ideas and words.

Is it the words she gives to me that convey the feelings
or is it feelings she sends to me that create the words
Words that I bend and twist into the material
I call my poem?

---

a thought

life is a lot like a yo-yo.
it has its ups and downs
but it takes practice
before you get it right

A Little Park

It's a little Park.
Not shiny and clean like the upscale row houses
on Sherbrook Street.
It's not polished marble and fresh mown grass.

It's more earthy, more common in flavor and class.
It's the park of the local folk with people at tables drinking
wine from bottles hidden inside plastic bags,
while others share bread crumbs with the pigeons.

It's a park where parents keep watchful eyes on
their children and menacing dogs on a leash.
It's a park were the people from the low rent tenements
come to share their misery and their joy and the cleaning
staff from the hospital come to take their smoke breaks.

Lovers kiss and dream about how their love
will shape a different kind of life
ignoring the angry yells from the wine drinkers
over who is taking more.
And the strutting drug dealers who never sit down.

It's the park were the servants and the servers
of the working class joke and laugh to ignore the struggles
and pains of eking out an existence
while sharing with others who know what it is to struggle.
They ignore the feelings of powerlessness
and hide their anger from each other.

It's a Park where life lives at a level
that we of the privileged class prefer to be
only peripherally aware.
It's a little Park on Ste. Catherine's street in Montreal.

We Speak

We speak with our animal voice.
We see through our animal eyes
We hear with our animal ears and bite with our animal teeth.
Our animal bodies move to the beat of the drum we call life.
Seeing ourselves as beings; separate from each other,
is animal thinking.
Our downfall is that too many of us think
from our animal brain

Tribalism is animal thinking
Nationalism is animal thinking
Those who cannot speak our tribal language
become the other.
Those who do not follow our tribal customs
become the other.
Those not of our tribal religion also become the other.

A sense of inner peace arises from unconditionally
loving my own humanity.
Then I can see the common experience shared by us all
and my life is reflected in everyone I meet.
When I see the world through spiritual thinking,
World Peace can begin.

When we view the world from a spiritual mind
World peace can begin.
When we experience the world from
a one world perspective
World peace can begin.
When we accept our common humanity
and love ourselves unconditionally
World peace can begin.

We Speak Part II

How can I step outside the monkey brain
that dominates most of my thinking?
How can I think from the spiritual mind
when most of my thoughts are unseen?
They zoom past faster than a speeding bullet.
I totally miss many of the thoughts that drive my actions.

Awareness of the responsibility of one's actions
is spirit manifesting within the animal.
When the body is ill
it is the manifestation of an injured spirit.
Look to the emotions to tell us why.

Am I an animal that has acquired spiritual consciousness?
When did our primate ancestors become conscious?
Is this the story of Adam and Eve?
Why in that story is the gift of self-conscious
awareness blamed on the female.

The key is to be aware of the animal
that your spiritual being inhabits.
We borrow these animal bodies to have
Experiences in the physical world.
Becoming aware of the animal we inhabit
is the value of Mindfulness.

It's Only a Dollar

"It's Only a Dollar."
He tossed the words out as he passed me by.
It took a milli-second to cross space between us
as if he had thrown them at me.
He tossed the words out draped in disdain
as if he was throwing something away along
with the words. "It's only a dollar!"

The meta-message and body language conveyed
his scorn for such lowly money.
He was young and healthy had a job,
and contempt for the unimportant.
I had just passed two beggars sitting on the sidewalk
around the corner on 6th street asking for spare change.

The speaker may have noticed the beggars or may not have.
But he needed to look at the beggar man
who was offering his passer-by a gift.
the opportunity to feel compassion.
Not by giving him or her money

But the opportunity to recognize
the humanity in the Beggar-man
He or She has been loved as somebody's child,
somebody's lover, somebody's parent,
who have been defeated some-way, some-when, somehow.
They are not broken people;
but have taken on the role of a beggar offering a gift.

The gift of an opportunity to experience compassion
for our own humanity.
Let's not pretend we wish it not so but we all need
compassion for the wounds we carry.
For to be human is to have been hurt some-way,
some-when, some-how wounded by life itself.

The beggar needs to be thanked for taking on
this difficult role in this lifetime thereby giving us the
opportunity to learn compassion for ourselves.
And that's a bargain. After all;
It's only a dollar

You don't know me.

If you think you know me based on my clothes
or the colour of my skin
You don't know me

If you hear I speak with an accent
And assume I am an immigrant
You don't know me

If you think you know something about who I am
based on your assumptions we will never get to
know what wonderful people we both are.

Don't Look Away

Don't look away!
Why do you fear me?
Are you afraid to see that you too are a hungry wolf?
That we are both lone wolves hungering for love,
each in our own way.

I crave love that I will not; cannot allow.
I don't trust love, for its only pain when it leaves
And it always leaves.
And it always hurts

I want to be seen of value but I cannot allow it.
Better to believe I am not loveable
I don't want to be tricked by the promise of love
That unfulfilled promise that wounded me,
so deeply I cannot catch my own dinner
so I steal or extort or beg for the money
that will buy away the pain.

When did the wounding start?
In utero from a wounded womb?
In childhood from a wounded Mother and an ever absent Father.
Or as a youth from a wounded society made insane
by never-ending wars and the collateral damage
from its never-ending losses.

I am the beggar, the thief, the alcoholic, the dealer
I am the drug-addicted prostitute, the wife abuser, the murderer.
Or am I guilty of some unremembered crime
from centuries past and this is my karmic punishment?
I am society's tragedy and will pay any price
to exorcize the pain

And perhaps, before my addiction kills me,
I'll recover from this wound that afflicts me so.
And awaken to smell the rose.
See the beauty that surrounds me and the beauty that still lives,
hidden inside of me.

Teach the Little Ones

What we teach the little ones
When they are two and three and four
Is one thing and one thing only

Is this a safe world or an unsafe world?
This choice will shape everything
of their future life.

This observable truth
is a reflection of our own beliefs and
can be best seen from a point of awareness.

a thought

too often we sacrifice our inner child on
the altar of becoming grown up.

a thought

many of us are so good at lying
we can lie to ourselves and not even notice

Talk to the Child

What relieves the disappointments of life?
What heals the wounds of life's multitude of losses?
What mitigates the pain that life gives to our childhood?
Healing comes from processing those feelings.
Talk to the child.

Look past the reflection in the mirror
as the child you once were lives there still.
Day by day we grow older but buried emotions never
age. Anger, shame, sorrow, losses, soul injuries and
hurts to the heart are still there. Talk to the child.

All the unprocessed feelings from childhood are there
buried inside the wall protecting us from life's wounds.
Unprocessed emotions never die
They remain always there, always waiting to be mended
Talk to the child.

The adult part of youknows how to talk it out.
Our inner child hides behind the wall we built.
as protection from the inevitable hurts of life.
Our child lives there, with the wounding memories
Talk to the child.

That internal child is still very much alive.
That is where joy lives, and laughter and
moments of gleeful pleasure
Always ready to release the energy that is buried
among the pain.
You can't just ignore or brush it away.
Talk to the child

Talk to the child in you like a patient, understanding parent
Have compassion for the hurt, for the shame,
for the feelings of powerlessness.
Therein lies empowerment to live a life fulfilled.
Release the child from the unprocessed feelings
Talk to the child.

To be seen

I can't see
I'm not blind or anything
I just can't see me.

I've never really been seen by anyone.
I guess it's OK because my old man was a drunk all his life
and he lived to a ripe old age.

It feels like he used to beat on me every day
and call me a stupid waste of time and money until
I punched him in the face when I was 17.
We never spoke again.

Mom was long gone by then
And when I got caught lifting things she said
she barely had enough to take care of herself.
We never spoke again either.

I had plenty of odd jobs until I got me a steady job.
Worked in the mill until the drinking got to me.
Nothing steady since.
Except for this job standing outside the liquor store
Hoping to get enough to go inside and spend it.

---

a thought

there are those of us that are so good at judging others
that we can find them guilty
without even knowing what they did

Depression Drive is just past Loneliness Lane.

Sadness Street is just one street past Loneliness Lane with
Depression Drive located just a few blocks away.
They have shared this part of town for millennia
Each courting the believer of this unkind passion play

Insanity lurks in the dark alleys of this neighbourhood.
With Hatred and Violence Streets down by the docks
just beyond Judgment Row and Disapproving Avenue.
Again each one seducing their inhabitants to
a lower and lower vibration.

Vibrations so low and so heavy there is not else
but encroaching darkness.
It is hard to remember that once there was sunshine here.
Where have the neighbourhoods of love and peace and joy gone?
In what part of town do quiet and contentment still live?

From my childhood, I remember what it was like
living on Hardship Road
From there I had a view of both Poverty Lane and Depression Drive.
I observed the struggles and feelings of shame that exist there
By the grace and good luck, my visits to all these streets were short.

As a teen, I hid out for a while on Malcontent Row
which dead ends at Rebellion Park that s located between
Self-Importance Parkway and the No-Ethics Estates.
I looked and looked and each experience showed me the
life path for the characters. "No thanks, I remarked;
"I've read those scripts and I know the karma they carry.

Ignorance and Intolerance Streets are both ignorant and intolerable
but are often draped in facades of virtue and morality that are hidden
behind elegance and grace, but are actually neither.
I am grateful that I chose not to venture into these neighbourhoods.

Finally, I found what I had been looking for
It had been in my neighbourhood all the time.
I just didn't have the experience to recognize it.
I see now that Peace Avenue and Love Court reside within me no
matter what street I live on.

---

a thought

the motto of a rebellious child;
"It's always easier to get forgiveness
than it is to get permission."

---

a haiku

if parting be sweet
my sorrow tells truth to me
the pain is bitter

---

a thought

what does the pickpocket see
when he sees the Buddha?
the pickpocket can't see the Buddha.
he only sees those willing to be his victim.

Who Is She To You?
(A poem for Women's Day.)

Who is she to you?
A Mother who deserves your respect because she is your Mother.
The bearer and entry point to bring you into existence.

Who is she to you?
A wife, a life partner, a lover, an advocate,
someone who's got your back, while you and her try to sort thru the
pitfalls and convolutions of a relationship.

Who is she to you?
A daughter who merits your unconditional love
Not because she's perfect but because unconditional love
will teach her to love herself.

Who is she to you?
A sister who is there to drive you batty
and to suffer together the experience of the truly
crazy making parents that you share.

Who is she to you?
A teacher who treated you with kindness
when your playground experience was crumbling down
around your ears.

Who is she to you?
The sales clerk who's had a difficult day
with a world of kids, bosses and god knows what,
who deserves your patience because she's got a crummy job with
crummy pay and she's there to serve you.

Who is she to you?
She is someone who's been insulted, verbally abused, sexualized at
a young age and physically threatened at some time in her life just
because she's female.

Who is she to you?
A person who deserves nothing less than your full respect as an
equal human being. That's who she is to you!

a haiku

my love is wasted
on frivolous desires
it belongs to her.

a thought

i am sorry mother spider for destroying your web
but those blackberries are ripe and I'm a human
and it is the habit of humans to take whatever we want
and disregard whatever's in the way.

Ordinary Mary

Mary, Mary quite ordinary.
What were the dreams you dreamed?
And did any of them ever come to be true?
I never really knew you or what needs you had?
Whatever they might have been you kept them all to yourself
and I apologize because I never thought to ask.

Mary, Mary quite ordinary
I knew you were my Mother and that was all I knew of you.
It never occurred to me that you were a person too,
who had a life other than to be there just for me.
Tell me Mary, what was it that you aspired
to be or to do.

Mary, Mary quite ordinary
What were the thoughts you had as evolution
passed in the blink of an eye,
From oil lamp light to spacemen walking on the moon?
As a girl did you dream you were to be married,
bear children, live life, and grow old out on the farm?
The farm the bank took 'cause of the rains that never came.

Mary, Mary quite ordinary
I heard that times were tough when I was little
And whenever I was frightened
you took me to your rocking chair.
The one you rocked me in when you were frightened too.
As I grew older I labeled you as nothing fancy, nothing bold.
Just a housewife in the city with a family to look after.

Mary, Mary quite ordinary
For seven days and seven nights, the rains did constant fall
and again you lost your home.
Only it wasn't drought this time as the river overflowed
and swept away all of our possessions

and the memories that they held
afloat out on the lake just a mile or two away
but gone forever more.

Mary, Mary quite ordinary,
I know so little of who you might have been.
So now you're gone but not forgotten.
I wish I could tell you that you'll be in my heart forever.
and to thank you, oh so much, for being my ordinary Mother.

Rain

The beauty in the rain is expressed
as wild flowers on the hillside.
The gift in the rain is accessible
as the bounty on our table
Bemoan not the lack of sunshine
but rejoice in rain's gift of life.
For without the rain
You and I do not exist.

Jack

He was a showman through and through; talented and more.
and wounded deeply by the rules of his century.
Back then it was God, King and Country;
Children seen and not heard.
And no room for an opera singer
slinging hay and horse manure on a Manitoba farm.

It's a hard scrabble life, and you better know your place.
Ignore the drought, ignore the insanity of war,
and death in the millions.
Ignore the Spanish flu which killed your neighbour
and his parents too.
Ignore the bank's foreclosure
as you watched your prized horses sold by the auctioneer.
There is no such thing as trauma
and to process feelings of failure is not allowed.

There is no other place when you don't know any other.
He was a showman through and through; talented and
more; wounded deeply by the rules of his century.
A talented singer and actor working in an insurance office
trying hard not to notice that the life
of that desire had passed him by.

How do you cope with a world changing 1,000 times faster
than the societal structure into which you were born?
How do you transit from horse powered farming
to man on the moon and not be in shock?
How do you shift from 19th-century rules
to 20th century reality?

But thank you for struggling through it all to be there
and show me your dysfunctional coping ways.
Thank you for providing a place for me to grow.
Thank you for the gift of your food, your clothing
your shelter, and for ignoring my "you're not
perfect rage!" Thank you for doing your best in a
world struggling to keep pace with itself.
Thank you for being my Father.

Creation
(For my Father, written on the day he died)

I am Creation.
The primal forest was my birth.
I am here to the end

Cry not at my passing
For I have not died.
I am.

The streams, the forests,
the mountains, the earth,
are my soul, my being.

My existence as a being
Is here in the earth and
I shall rise again.

As long as trees grow and rivers flow
I cannot die.
The Earth is my spirit.
as long as the Earth lives
I will live.

Easter Parade

Take away religions use of this season
and see it as recognition of the birth of spring.
Then Easter becomes a true celebration of the renewal of life.

I sit among four blossoming cherry trees
Intermittently releasing petals that fall like large snowflakes,
covering the terrace in a pink-tinted blanket.

In my hand, I hold the ubiquitous Yellow Dandelion
Full and bright in the sunlight, its intensity begins to fade
as I lay it along the spine of my open book.

Somewhere behind me a white-capped chickadee beeps
out his value as he seeks a mate.
the DNA imperative meaning he knows not else to do.

Drops of rain interrupt my blissful Eden
causing me to seek shelter among the nearby pines
as the rain quickens and briefly turns to hail.

With distant thunder joining the audacious clouds
that intrude on the suns task to renew and replenish.
Thus Mother Earth announces her change of dress.

This has been the Easter's ritual repeated for millennia
This is mother earth at her rebirthing perfection.
Spring is here and life is renewed once more.

Wild Flowers on a Hillside

This earth is an amazing artistic creation.
The artist in me knows I could never be as good
as the artist that painted them … Gaia.
But I can word-paint the feelings that
observing nature shares with me.

I cannot voice the song that nature sings.
But I hear the song of the eagle's cry.
And I can hear the music of the pine forest
whispers on the wind.

Carve faces on a mountain are spectacular
But mankind's contribution to the earth's
beauty is minuscule;
compared to what the Mother Earth provides.

There is little to compare with the majestic
beauty of a snow-capped mountain.
The majestic view of a million, million stars
the beauty of mountains, forests, waterfalls,
lakes, deserts and
wild flowers on a hillside.

A Day at the Beach

The slanted rays of the sun glisten like plated silver reflected off the roiling sea. Crashing waves began tossing spray while still distant from the shore, diminishing in size as they climb to meet the beach

A trio of pelicans skim along a trough between the waves. Occasionally rising up to wheel and dive headlong into the chaotic sea only to reappear moments later back in flight having captured its quarry or not.

Piercing the sand with its long curved beak the Curlew searches the dregs of the remnant waves looking for morsels of something driven ashore by the sea and the wind.

A hundred tiny winged arrows speed past inches above the sand, flashing a white underside. They turn in perfect unison as of one mind; then alighting and launching into an immediate search for food.

On the breeze, a pair of gulls glide on stilled wings to a casual landing, then pick and pull among the clumped patches of seaweed discovering and consuming small unseen creatures.

A dogfish shark lay on its side buffeted by the remnant waves. Occasionally thrashing in protest to its imminent demise. And whose carcass will eventually feed the gulls, the crows and the majestic sea eagle that awaits atop the pine just off the beach.

Did any one of these creatures pause to consider questions of life and death? Did any one of them ponder on the purpose of their life? Did any one of them consider praying to God to spare their life or request the good fortune of a bumper crop?

This is Gaia in her most honest portrayal of the cycle of nature. It is life and death being acted out in this microcosm of the world. This is Nature in her truest form; that of the continual feeding of something off of something else.

This is a day at the beach.

Just 30 Miles
(A first responder's lament)

Just 30 miles to Baba's house
Just 30 miles to loving safety
The day was sunshine and soft winds
Take your time no need to be hasty

Three days since the family left Winnipeg
Time to show Baba the golden-haired angel child
Just 30 miles to Montreal and Baba's waiting arms
All the way the weather had been fair and mild.

With Baba anxiously awaiting
To greet her child's unmet offspring
The newest arrival in the family
With the priest at the ready to do the anointing

She was three and on her way to Baba's house
The warming sun made it time to take a nap
Along the way passing fields and farms
Innocent and fast asleep she lay on Mother's lap

A little anxious to get there before dark
As he passed the car ahead; hells' chaos erupted,
and in an instant a child was dead.
Beyond belief; love's Universe afflicted.

With sunbeams glinting off the mortuary table
In perfect innocence, angelic there she lay
I deeply drank from that wellspring of sadness
brought about by the events of the day.

On a mild summer's day death stalked the highway.
Offering sleep from which she will never arouse
adding echoes of grief for those left to mourn.
with just 30 miles to Baba's house

It's Not the Path

If ever anyone tells you they know the path
that will ease the pain of living.
It's not the path.
Say Thank you and pass by.

If ever anyone promises you they know the path
that will save you from eternal death.
It's not the path.
Say Thank you and pass by.

If someone says you that you will burn in Hell
If you don't follow their only true Path
That's not the path.
Say Thank you and pass by.

If ever offered the secret of the magic that will open
the entrance to the garden of Eden
It's not the path.
Say Thank you and pass on by.

If the offered Path feels dark and foreboding pay attention.
Darkness is never the Path to Light
Say thank you and pass on by.

Should someone tell you they know what you need
to heal that pain within. That cannot be.
Only you have the key to your healing
Politely say thank you but pass on by

If ever you are tempted to look outside of yourself
to have someone show you the Path.
It's never going to be the path
Say Thank you to the thought and pass it by

The only place where the Path exists,
The Path where joy dwells and all healing takes place;
the path of intention.
That path of intention is within you.
Create the intention and your true Path will find you.

Ozymandias is Not My Name

Fame and fortune are as fleeting as time itself.
It seems I have always known the seduction
hidden in the ideas that I am this or I am that.
The timelessness of the soul is not defined
by such things mortal

We exist in a self-devouring passion play.
It matters not what I have or what I leave behind
What I seek are life's hidden treasures.
And regardless of tides make a mark in the sand.

I see no sadness in death
but a doorway to the next adventure
Is my life's close the end of this chapter,
or the end of the book?

---

a thought

trust those who say they are seekers of truth
trust not, those who claim to have found it!

The Monk

He knew every chant
He knew every prayer
He practiced his mantra based meditation daily
He knew the healing mudra finger positions
for both one hand and for two hands.

He could raise his kundalini energy
until his whole body vibrated in breathtaking ecstasy.
He could transport his awareness to the craters
of the moon
or wander through the planets of distant stars.
But the veil of death was closed to him.

He knew all the teachings by heart and could recite
the dogma in his sleep but still the question remained;
What happens to his consciousness when his body dies?
Would his awareness of the self, cross that last barrier?
Would he recognize himself and still
know himself as separate?

Or when he merged into the One mind would all traces
of his identity that defines him as separate, disappear?.
Would all traces of his individuality be obliterated
so that his cherished "I am" no longer existed,
and along with it, his ability to feel emotion?

In this existence, we can experience joy and love and
compassion and with it the potential for the depths of
sadness and for anger and for fear.
He understood there must be contrast for to
only feel one feeling is to not feel at all.

And if at death the emotions of love, of joy, of
compassion vanish and along with it the contrasting
emotions of fear, anger and sorrow also disappear?
He asked; "Is it only through this body
that we experience emotions?"

Is eternal bliss so boring that we incarnate
in order to experience the contrast?
Are we here for the range of feelings from
the highs of joy to the lows of sorrow?
He saw that without this contrasting range,
life could not fulfill its purpose

His conclusion was that life needs to have this
roller-coaster of emotions
that uses the highs and the lows to let us know
we are alive.
And in the end, our resolute Monk concluded
that the simple purpose of life is to enjoy the ride.

---

a haiku

my heart longs to know
what lies beyond deaths' door.
will love greet me there

The Shadow

It sits on my left shoulder.
Totally mute; saying nothing, always waiting.
Always there when I allow its presence felt.

It waits; it waits, this shadow of death.
It waits to be the guide through the last portal.
This last passageway to the next adventure.

I twist my head to catch a glimpse
And look death square in the face.
Ever the shadow it hides behind my ear; ever the secret.

It is felt as a grip that wants to draw my shoulders together.
A cringe sensation around my heart as it readies the adrenaline
to fuel the fight or flight response.

Where are my addictions to distract me from this pursuer?
Where is my ignorance to ease this awareness
of the unpredictability of death?
Where is my belief that somehow
I will escape this ultimate treachery?

Nothing can distract me from the knowledge
that death awaits me.
Still the shadow waits.
Waits until the end of time.
the end of my time.

Forgiveness

As with everything in the Universe
True forgiveness begins in the heart that is looking inward,
and it must, like charity, begin at home.

When I forgive myself right down to my core belief
my life begins to get better.
I begin to look after my needs, wants and desires.

I'm still open and loving but I see that in some situations
there was confusion.
What's the right decision? What will gain me the most love?
Like most of us, I am always looking to be loved more.

But when I forgive myself
I learn I am enough! Just as I am, I am enough
I want but don't need the affection of others
so that I feel loved.
I don't need to have power over others
or give others my power.

I just am. And that's OK.
Joy is in not only, not minding the pain of living
but is in actually recognizing all as part of the gift of life.

Without the capacity for contrast, there can be no joy.
Without the occasional grief, there is no contrast.
Eventually one can see the light and the dark are the same.
They are called experiences.

How Dare You Write Poetry?

Can you hear him? I can. He's the voice in my head that said;
"How dare you write poetry?" It was clear and distinct.
"How dare you write poetry?"
The voice continued; "Stop! Stop! This is not good for you!"
"Interesting," I thought, as I sat down to write this poem.

Whose voice is that?
It sounds stern like a man voice
But whether Father's voice or Mother's voice,
it simply doesn't matter.
They both reside inside my head

Wanting to tell me where the unsafe boundaries begin.
Boundaries that pretend, if followed, will keep me safe.
How effective are those boundary voices then?
That is fallacy: because it's not true:
no matter how safe we play it, in the end, we all die.

Maybe the purpose of the voices, as primitive as they are,
is to keep the monkey alive long enough so it can procreate.
The Goddess of procreation is the owner of the voice
heard inside the inner sanctum of my mind.

For a million, million years that voice has urged us to survive.
Follow the rules and live.
"Here!" God said as she splatters sticky, gooey protoplasm
across the cooling Earth.
"Go forth and multiply and see what you can make of that."
That edict has been driving every species
to procreate ever since.

This is the paramount edict of existence that drives all species.
Keep surviving and evolving through reproduction
Parents become parents who become parents
who become parents,
changing microbially in accord with conditions.
Until perhaps one day we can say to God
"Mother, this is what we made of it."

Every species exists because of the voices
from the primitive mind.
Instructions that strive to ensure continuation of the seed.
Variations of these rules have been passed down
century after century.
But boundaries deter our need to grow.

So why is it not safe to write poetry?
Because it is not safe to stand out among the crowd
They might see my imperfections.
For a hyper-narcissistic introvert like me
Standing naked and unashamed before the world
is the most life-threatening thing there is to do.

But there is another voice, a more urgent voice,
a louder voice that says expand, grow; defy the rules,
defy the boundaries and express the voice.
Express the voice from the other side that
demands to speak its' truth
Share the knowledge that it is time to move
from animal-based rules of greed, lust and desire for more
Time to move to a life of awareness,

Awareness that comes from the heart
supported by our emotions
Awareness that allows us to see just how difficult it is to exist
as a spiritual being living in an animal body
with that voice that tells me the rules to be safe.
How dare I write poetry? "I do because I must."
And that voice is mine.

Siddhartha by the River

I am Siddhartha by the river
Surrounded by beauty;
living quiet in peace.
Contemplating the many gifts of the Universe

I am Siddhartha by the river.
Meditating on the delicate essence of internal peace,
that arrive only in small moments,
amid the fury and frenzy of the day.

I am Siddhartha by the river.
Cautious about which thought is a teaching
And even more cautious
about which thought is a seduction.

I am Siddhartha by the river.
Noting that all dogma with their myths and vested,
interests have inaccurately guessed at the truth.
So there is no true teacher who can show me the way.

I am Siddhartha by the river.
Seeking to follow the path, where there is no path
Concluding that there is no route to enlightenment,
save my own.

I am Siddhartha by the river.
Amazed at the life story people create out of their
myths, beliefs and experiences; then blame the other,
unable to see themselves as both cause and effect.

I am Siddhartha by the river.
Wanting to be humble and knowing that wanting
is always a distraction from the now.
Wanting to be wise and knowing
that too is a deviation from the now.

I am Siddhartha by the river.
Believing life is a river; ever emerging, ever-changing,
even becoming new, flowing
from experience to experience to experience.

I am Siddhartha by the river.
Watching all things attempt to seduce my ego
by telling me I am apart and separate from the other.
Watching the connectedness of all things, and
observing that the river and the forest
come together through me.

I am Siddhartha by the river
Watching the creation and then the passing of all things
Seeing that, without the light and the dark,
life is without purpose.

I am Siddhartha by the river
Grateful that within this Universe
there is the presence of love.
While waiting to die and do it all over again.

I am Siddhartha by the river.

The "NOW"

Nothing in the now matters.
But there is only the now.
Therefore nothing matters
Is it all an illusion anyway?

Nothing in the now matters
The now never happens.
'caus by the time we observe it;
it's already history

Nothing matters in the now,
There is only the now
But it lives for less than the blink of an eye
and is gone.

Nothing matters in the now
It's only light that has slowed
to manifest a material world of matter;
A place where we experience emotion.

What matters is the story we tell
to give us the emotions that we feel.
Can we manifest a now
that is different from the now just passed?

But there is only the now
Each now with its own set of rules and beliefs
that creates the next now.
Can we manifest that as a now of love?

We build our lives
Based on a foundation of trauma;
The wound that we all carry,
that we are mortal beings

Nothing in the now matters.
Except that we love our life as it is;
not as it should be
and love ourselves without condition.

The Eyes of My Poetic Soul

When we view the world through the eyes of our poetic soul
We see the oneness of all that is.
We see the mountain in the pebble in the hand
We see the tree in the seed of the Oak,
We see the river in a drop of water
and the ocean in the rain.

When we see the world through the eyes of the poetic soul
We see the white in the black of Yin
and the black in the white of Yang
Our humanity is the instrument that allows our soul
to show us the infinite perfection of the Universe

When we look at the self through the eyes of our poetic soul,
We need not hide behind our excuses and our addictions.
There is no need to dwell on what might have been,
rather celebrate the joy of what was and what is!
and see that within every experience is a gift of love.

We can see the beauty and the perfection of our humanity.
With no need to carry a yoke of limitations
no need to carry a burden of guilt or of
shame that we are both imperfect and impermanent.

When we see ourselves through the eyes of our poetic soul
We realize that this life is the opportunity to awaken
to the truth of all that we really are.
For at death we will look directly into the
eyes of our soul and see eternity.

A Happy Place

Find me a place
where Mother Earth lives
for I will be happy there.

Find me a place
where the pine trees whisper their song
and I will be happy there.

Find me a place where nature is alive and well.
where cool streams flow and stillness prevails.
for I will be happy there.

Find me a place where winter means snow and cold
and crisp, clear starlight nights,
Find me a place where fireweed blossoms in the spring,
and gentle summer breezes blow.

Then bury me there in that place
for I will be happy there.

a quote

"birth is not the beginning
death is not the end"
Zhuangzi (Chuang Tzu)
370 BCE – 287 BCE

Part Five

Stories

To the Other Side

We sail within a vast sphere, ever drifting into uncertainty...

Blaise Pascal circa 1648

To the Other Side

Chapter One

This ancient used up body that for nearly a century has carried him from experience to experience, from adventure to adventure, was about to expire.

From his bed he looked towards the sunshine and the trees just outside the window; he thought, "I'm going to miss this!" "I think this time I've bought the farm" he whispered.

"What farm?" She asked.

"Heh!" he coughed a small dry cough; "the one you're going to bury me under. Heh!" He coughed again. His cough was soft as he had no strength in it. His remaining life energy was quickly dissipating.

After a pause to take a breath he continued; "What do you think this is all about?" he struggled to lift his head to see her more clearly. She moved her chair closer to his bed.

"All what is about? you mean life?"

He stopped struggling and let his head fall back to the pillow. He closed his eyes and spoke; "It seems to me life is; my life, was a waste. What are we creating with this insanity we call life? There was no defined goal! No purpose! Someone wrote that life is full of sound and fury signifying nothing!"

He struggled to find the energy to keep breathing.

"Shakespeare." she paused, "it's from Macbeth."

"Damn it; I'm as near to dying as one can get and in spite of my life long efforts to find a reason for life, I still don't understand why we are here. Why are we born, what's in it of value? We are takers, not givers"

He went to wave his hand in a sweeping gesture but couldn't. He could still think but his body was reluctant to contribute to the conversation.

She responded; "I thought you believed the purpose of life was to add the experience you gained in life's to the knowledge of the Universe." She urged. "I remember you talked about adding your experiences in order to expand consciousness, the consciousness of the Universe. You saw that as important work and you certainly had a life filled with experiences." I think you should be proud."

"But why? Seems to me life is…" he broke off.

She waited. Waited, watching his chest for signs of breath. She had been here every day since the last heart attack and every day she noticed his breath was getting more and more shallow. The energy that sustained his body was failing. "He's had a good long life." She thought to herself. "Now it's time to pay the ferryman to take him across the river. I guess death is a fair price to pay for the chance to have a life.

Barely audible, he wheezed. "a waste." and took another breath.

He never heard her supportive words. His mind had drifted away from the conversation and turned inward. He wondered to himself, "Is there really such a thing as a death rattle?"

He hadn't yet noticed the gradually increasing sound of the wind that grew steadily louder. Oblivious to the increasing uproar he wondered; "If there is a death rattle? Will I hear it when I croak?"

He had often listened to a spiritual teacher known as Abraham and he very much liked her disrespectful reference to dying as croaking. He liked the word; *croak*. It seemed to take the sting out of the notion of death.

That train of thought was ended by the distractingly loud noise and increasing darkness. His focus centered on the effort it took to take the next breath. His breathing was so shallow he wondered if he had taken it yet.

He hadn't. He had taken his last breath.

The noise stopped.

Silence! There was absolute silence. There was absolute darkness. The first thing he noticed that told him he had passed into death was the constant tug of gravity was missing.

He floated in the silence and the darkness. Funny he thought; "I expected to be floating somewhere up near the ceiling looking down on my last mortal remains, but nothing. No heavenly hosts, no choirs of angels; no bountiful floral gardens full of relatives waiting to greet me."

Realizing he had left his body he considered that he was now without a specific identity and he was only a thought. With a slight chuckle, he mused; "Thought! Thou shalt be known henceforth as Thought."

Now that the howling wind had ceased there was only silence; silence and darkness.

Chapter Two

The light began as a tiny, sparkly diamond, a glimmer of light. He had the sense the glimmer was either very small or very far away.

Thought realized it was rapidly increasing in size and he speculated; "is this light approaching me or am I falling into it."

As the sparkling light grew Thought perceived a distinctive edge which gave the light a disc shape with a defined edge to it and beyond this edge was total darkness.

The gleaming hard edge rim that divided darkness and the light flashed by him at speed annihilating the darkness. As it passed came another enormous roar and an intensity of light that obliterated any possibility of shadows. The light seemed to be emanating from every direction so there were no shadows, no variations of any kind. Everything was immersed in white light!

Light illuminates whatever is present but colour is a reflection of the vibration that emanates from the object. Here, although no material substances exist the light was so intense it was as though a fog of brightness had descended with intense whiteness everywhere! Here again, there was silence.

There was no sense of a passage of time but eventually, the brightness dimmed and, as it did, stars began to appear. Then galaxies and finally his consciousness emerged floating in space no longer embodied but now simply a point of energy; simply a thought.

Thoughts' mind reached out for his persona markers to orient himself to this new environment. Fear was building in his thoughts as all traces of ethnicity, all identifying culture, religion, race the other stories that incarnates tell themselves that make up the, *I am.*

Those persona markers were no longer there. All the stories that grew over a lifetime of temporal experiences and their accompanying emotions were gone. All was stripped away. The symbols he used to orient and identify who he was were absent.

Chapter Three

In the light, he sensed a presence.

"Welcome home," said Awareness. "Your emanations tell me that you had a good journey. I can feel you got to have all the experiences that you had hoped for. Your aura gleams with the experiences of positive energy that you bring with you from the other side

Ignoring Awareness, Thought examined his thinking. He seemed lucid and coherent and for a moment he considered the possibility that he was not dead but dreaming. Even so, he didn't have the sensations of being in body. To Thought, what had seemed so real began to fade and became ...*this place.* It felt vaguely familiar to Thought, he asked. "What is this place?"

"The stars and galaxies are yours. This is your expectation of what the after death experience should look like. This is your idea of what it was going to be like after you disembodied.

Many have the expectation this is a garden of sorts. This is your version of heaven. Here we are in a Universe of pure energy, absolute potential with nothing material until you make it so.

This is the etheric realm. One step removed from the physical realm you just left."

"How is it that I can think?"

"All you ever were is a thought and it's all you ever will be. In this realm you were never born and you will never die. You are as we all are; conscious energies with several levels of expression.

Although we are ultimately only one, we exist within one or more of the seven Universes connected through a line of energy that runs from Source; Supreme Being, Universal Energy, God, Brahman, Ra or whatever name you choose from the thousands of names, to where you exist now in this Etheric Universe.

You are also connected through each of the six other levels and when incarnated, to a physical body.

At each level we are always a complex combination of the individual energy and the divine. The connecting energy through the seven Universes is known as the soul, the Atman, so that, at every level, we are connected to Source energy through the soul.

Our soul, like the divine, was never born and can never die and we can move at will through each level depending on what is our perceived need to add to consciousness. All entities existing or not existing are energies seeking to know what who and what we are. This is a quest to know and experience infinity.

"If you remember you and several other souls agreed on a list of experiences that all believed would benefit the consciousness of the Universe by adding a number of experiences. Then through your manifested embodiments, all your energies proceeded to create that story.

Your returning energy says that you accomplished all your goals and brought back all the emotional energies you had hoped to gain from the embodiment experience.

Those are important experiences and additions to the consciousness of the Universe that were your objectives.

Thought protested; "Objectives? Did I have an agenda? I am not quite sure I understand. Was I sent there to capture and retrieve emotional energies? Did I just go through the turmoil and contortions of a lifetime so that I could bring back experiences so that some cosmic entity could grow and expand?"

Awareness interjected; "Not sent…"

Thought ignored Awareness' interruption; "Is this correct? I had a purpose? Was I just sent to incarnate in human form, struggle through the painful ups and downs called life and then suffer through old age, sickness and death just so some higher being can have the thrill of having all of life's emotions but not have to deal with the gooey, messy reality of physical existence?"

With added energy to his communications Thought continued; "This sounds as though this Source energy character is an emotion leach. And in the process, God, or whatever the name is of this Spirit/me connection, so loves the world that it uses humans as slave labourers to do all the heavy emotional lifting that it takes to survive life and this Being can then add to its roster of experiences and not have to get down in the dirt with the human animals.

"Not sent!" Awareness hesitated to let the words sink in. "Not sent!" Awareness repeated. "Perhaps you can remember that you are both the creator and the created. It is you who choose to be the explorer and at the same time be the explored.

"Through incarnation, all involved were given, a chance to explore all possible experiences, a chance to explore infinity. You were successful and had a world of experiences and along with the wisdom gained through those understandings, you brought back all the loving energy that had been shared among those you engaged.

"Explore the idea that all the experiences you had were gifts. None of them were good and none of them were bad and that they were all just experiences you chose in order to experience the contrast. The gift in every one of them was another chance to learn and to grow.

This spirit world, while in itself is a gift, is eternal love. There is no contrast to learn from. Here, everything is complete. No past, no future, just now, and then now, and then now and then now. When we choose to incarnate we are given the opportunity to learn from the contrast and grow in wisdom and grow in compassion.

The contrast experienced in space-time activates the emotions and through experiencing emotions we expand the collective that is Universal love. You are a part of Universal Source energy and your understandings add to Universal consciousness."

"The Source Energy of the Universe is known by a thousand names in a thousand tongues; The One, The Source,

The Father of the Universe and its Mother and includes all entities corporeal, non-corporeal and other.

Everything in this Universe is a part of the One and we are all a part of the collective, the consciousness of all that is becoming aware of itself."

Awareness concluded. "Without the emotions added by humankind there is no reason for the Universe to exist. Human emotions are the source energy that creates the Universe Consciousness, knowledge of the self, is the essence and goal of all spiritual practice."

Thought began to shake off the limitations inherent in the story he had concluded about what life is about. As the idea expanded he became aware of the value of life, that life's experiences offered contrast. Contrast provides experiences and those experiences were the reason for life.

Thought reasoned; "I took embodiment as animated life to experience the contrast. And I suspect there are really only two energies; love and fear, life is really about the contrast between love; that is, light and fear; that is darkness. Of course! The purpose of life is about the conflict between the energy of light and the energy of darkness. It is through consciousness that light will overcome the darkness of fear.

And all of humanity are fully enfranchised participants in the process of a growing enlightenment with the intention of becoming light itself. The purpose of life is to learn how to create the story that brings happiness and a life of joy. Joy is love and love is light and light banishes fear, the darkness. The purpose of humanity is to bring love and light into the Universe and create a Universe based on unconditional love. The hidden gifts in the contrast are lessons in love"

Still bodiless, Awareness smiled.

Chapter Four

Standing near the back of the funeral parlour room, two mourners chatted about the recently departed; "I understand he's to be cremated.

"What's to be done with his ashes?" The other mourner asked.

"His son promised to take his Dad for a ride on his new Harley motorcycle and to scatter the ashes at a lakeside somewhere up in Northwestern Ontario."

"God, that sounds a real heavy trip. On the other hand it sounds like too much fun. Can you imagine; riding free in the wind with a task that has some profound purpose to it!"

"I hear also that he has not only to take the box of ashes but is also lugging a 40-pound headstone with him to leave by the lake. I like what's chiseled into it. There are no names, no dates. Just three words…"

THE ADVENTURE CONTINUES.

A note to my readers;
Thank you

Bio: Neall Ryon

Born in 1940 Neall Ryon can truly be considered a Renaissance man. Since he heard Socrates' maxim that an unexamined life is a wasted life, Neall has focused on seeking to understanding life.

Apart from being a perennial student of life his work history includes a variety of careers as a research manager, a business consultant, a business owner, a teacher, a husband, a father, a wanderer, a poet and for about a year, the co-host of a radio show on CFRO; World Poetry Café. As well, one of his poems; "Easter Parade" was selected to be included among the 150 poems celebrating Canada's 150th Birthday in the book Multicultural Creative Writing Collection

In his travels throughout the world and his wanderings though a life of adventure sought to answer the question; "What is there in life that is real and meaningful?" He concluded that a meaningful path was not to be found in the experiences of life's external offerings but in seeking out the truth that hides within each of us. Apparently it's not what you do in life that gives our life meaning, it's how you live it.

Contact and a few recent examples of his poetry can be found at "http://www.fromtheotherside.ca/"
www.fromtheotherside.ca

"Mr. Ryon listens to the Universe and with his talent, presents Its magic and wonder with passion. His pieces are insightful, inspiring and spiritually satisfying."

Sunny Beley B.A.Sc.

"I love reading Neall Ryon's work. Every story and every poem carries a message about life with many truths within his work. Neall looks at life and existence from a very special place. For those who are seeking for a meaning in life, in the world around and within themselves, I highly recommend reading Neall Ryan's book, From the Other Side."

Deborah L. Kelly,
Author, Through My Eyes, Heartworks, Cry of Humanity
Recipient, Writer's International Network Award.
Distinguished Writer International Award.

"Neall Ryon's book From the Other side is a deeply appreciated antidote to the ever present banalities that pass for conversations and observations in personal encounters and social media postings. I am grateful that he has been willing to share his exploration for what there is in life that is real and meaningful. This is a book in which every entry offers deep reflection and offer thoughts that merit your undivided attention."

Kit Racette: Montreal, Canada
Alexander Technique teacher associated with ATI
Alexander Technique International.
Grief Edu-therapist and Death Cafe facilitator
Trainer in Wholebody Focusing recognized
by Focusing Institute

Printed in the United States
By Bookmasters